Chef Karen Anne Murray's Tea Table

Dedication

for my parents, Eddison and Melrose
and for Melrose, Eloise, Eddison, Anthony, and Melinda
Will, Thomas and Marie, Betsy, Earl and Joseph
My nieces and nephews ... family

Pacific Grove's Purple Carpet

Acknowledgments

A special thank you to ...

My cherished husband Tom and son Andrew who have loved, supported me, edited, taste tested, critiqued and assisted in countless ways throughout this project. True comfort you both are.

Mum, Dad, sisters and brothers, our everlasting faith, your kindness, generosity, encouragement and forever love.

Patricia Hamilton, for your vibrancy and literary expertise.

Josie Cowden, you recipe tested with love and friendship in your heart and kindly edited each and every page.

My niece, Sophia Sorenson, for your glowing sunshine and photographic energy!

Raūl Nava, for years of food writing to encourage small-business growth and stability through your work.

Countless staff, clients and customers throughout the years, your support means so very much.

Family and friends around the world, you make me smile.

The smartphone made this project possible.

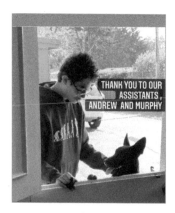

Sophia and Karen

Photo by Josie Cowden

Chef Karen Anne Murray's Tea Table

Softcover ISBN 978-1-953120-18-2

I-Book ISBN 978-1-953120-26-7

Copyright © 2021 Karen Anne Murray

ALL RIGHTS RESERVED

Hardcover ISBN 978-1-953120-25-0

Printed and bound in the U.S.A

www. eddisonandmelrose.com

tea@eddisonandmelrose.com

Photos by Karen Anne Murray and Sophia Sorenson except where noted

Design and production by Patricia Hamilton

Published by Pacific Grove Books, an imprint of Park Place Publications, Pacific Grove, CA 93950

Contact the author for special events, appearances, and bulk sales for groups.

TEA TABLE CONTENTS

Acknowledgments   2

Contents   3

Foreword   4

Table Introduction   6

About This Book   8

Shopping List   9

How to make a perfect cuppa!   10

Teatime   12   Teatime Menus   13

Contributors   52

TEA TABLE RECIPES

Celery Leaf Soup	17
Butter Lettuce Salad	19
Sausage Rolls	21
Tea Sandwiches	22
Curried Chicken Salad Tea Sandwich Filling	24
Cucumber Cream Cheese Tea Sandwiches	25
Sundried Tomato Bacon Tea Sandwich Filling	26
Joan's Kickin' Chickin' (JKC)	28
Fresh Breadcrumbs	28
Spinach Quiche	31
E&M Heart–Smart Lemon Curd	32

E&M West Coast Scones	33
Scone Cream	35
Queen Cakes	37
Queen Cake Cream	38
Butter Cookies	41
Karen Anne's Everyday Granola Parfait	43
Karen Anne's Soiree Granola Parfait!	43
French Toast Bites	45
Strawberry Lemonade	47
The E&M MoTeaTo	49
TeaMosa	50

Foreword
by Raúl Nava

Chef Karen Anne Murray's
Tea Table

Life is busy and hectic.

Each morning starts with a list of tasks. As the hours tick and tock, we nick away at our assignments one by one, yet by sunset, the list seems to have grown longer. Day in and day out, we plod along through our routine in a high-tech, wired world. In theory, this innovation brings us closer together, but in practice we've never been farther apart.

Modern life leaves us starved for escape and connection—more so in the face of a global pandemic.

Chef Karen Anne Murray invites us to purposefully pause, reflect, and reconnect by taking a seat at her tea table.

I was first introduced to Karen when she opened Eddison & Melrose in Monterey, California, in 2009. Named in honor of her parents and leveraging Karen's culinary training in England and globe-trotting experience as a restaurant chef, caterer, and personal chef, Eddison & Melrose brought proper afternoon tea to California's Central Coast.

Stepping into her cozy tea room and sitting down for a spot of tea and treats whisked me away from the bustling strip mall to the rolling hills of the English countryside. Her move to the corner of a shopping center in Pacific Grove expanded Eddison & Melrose to include granola, scones, and other baked goods.

My life was upended by a global pandemic last year, but I have frequently found sanctuary in Karen's baked delights. Several Saturdays have started with a visit to Eddison & Melrose to pick up her sublime scones—wonderfully light and buttery, finished with generous dollops of lemon curd, cream, and seasonal fruit jam, and of course enjoyed alongside a pot of bright, fragrant Eddison & Melrose royally inspired tea.

Tea is steeped in tradition in countries across the globe—a simple cup of water and leaves belies a complex cultural significance.

In Karen's homeland of England, tea borders on ritual. Afternoon tea emerged in the nineteenth century as a mid-afternoon meal of delicate delights like sandwiches, scones, and cakes among the upper class. (While most outside the United Kingdom use "afternoon" and "high" tea interchangeably, the latter is in fact a working-class meal of strong tea and savories enjoyed after a hard day's labor.)

Busy lives find afternoon tea now saved for special occasions, but Karen revives the tradition as an everyday escape, a reminder to stop and savor the little things, to take a bit of respite amidst the hustle and bustle of the day's chores.

Tea on its own is restorative, of course, but the true power of tea is its ability to brew connection to place, to people, and, perhaps most importantly, to ourselves.

We're privileged that Karen has shared her recipes for recreating teatime treats at home. She transports us to her childhood home in England, where a hot cuppa staved off the cold, wet West Midlands winters and offered a bit of joyful brightness no matter the season.

So put the kettle on, pour a cuppa, and take time to relax at Karen's tea table.

Raúl Nava is a freelance writer who has covered dining and restaurants across California's Central Coast for more than 10 years. His work has appeared in *Edible Monterey Bay*, the *Monterey County Weekly*, and the *Monterey Herald*.

Table Introduction

I don't recall the first time I noticed a free household item sitting outside all alone. In recent years, I smile as I drive through neighborhoods and see a loveseat, bookshelf or some other household item on the curb all forlorn. I smile because I think of someone who may have got out of bed that morning thinking it would be nice to have a chair in their garden on which to sit and relax. Then miraculously as that same person drives to the farmers market they notice a rattan chair outside a house with a piece of paper saying *free!*

These small miracles and simple pleasures in life bring me true joy! One morning on my way to work, I noticed a small wicker table outside a house. Later that day as my family and I went home from celebrating my sister's birthday, I drove by to see if the table was still there. It was. It was meant for me! Now, weeks later, here I am writing the cookbook I have dreamed of, and my stage is that same table.

Welcome to Tea Table

On this very table is where I hope to inspire,
encourage and awaken new creativity in you all!
—*Chef Karen Anne*

I enjoy seeing what you create
using the recipes from this book. Follow us on fb
and Instagram, and share photos @eddisonandmelrose

My free wicker table.

About This Book

I have purposely created these recipes with your good health in mind. One does not typically think of teatime as a healthy meal. Some of these recipes are a full-force splurge with butter, cream, sugar and more! Others I have toned down, realizing they are recipe staples for your everyday pantry.

When I work as a personal chef for my clients, my goal has always been to strive to prepare meals that are healthy enough to be enjoyed every day of the year. You may think that Lemon Curd is rich, and typically it is. The Heavenly Lemon Curd I created for the Tea Cottage is indeed that. The recipe for Lemon Curd included in this book will give you a Vitamin C boost for your heart and well-being that may be enjoyed daily and go well with the buttery-rich scone recipe you will find within these pages.

Not one to have a recipe next to me as I cook, I tend to memorize a method and glide through the kitchen in a similar way to my mother who is not a recipe follower. I add this, splash in that, and finish a dish off with a garnish, often thinking of my dad's green thumb as I do. Creating the recipes for the Tea Cottage, which has kept our customers from around the globe coming back for more, took time. Ultimately these recipes are a part of my being.

On these pages are newly created concoctions that keep you, the home chef or professional, in mind. My goal is to provide ease within your culinary endeavors with the hope that you too will make these recipes often.

HELPFUL SUBSTITUTIONS

butter – margarine or olive oil

all-purpose flour – oat flour - almond flour

milk – almond milk

granulated sugar – maple syrup or honey

Shopping List

You will find that most ingredients that are used for the recipes are basic and can easily be found at your local grocery store. Some items are seasonal. Here is a comprehensive list of what you will need to make any or all of the recipes within this book.

Pantry

all-purpose flour -
    oat or almond flour
baking powder
olive oil
cooking spray
powdered sugar
sugar -
    honey or
    maple syrup
walnuts
raisins
tea
balsamic vinegar
mustard
food coloring
sundried tomatoes
cocoa powder
vanilla flavoring
vegetable broth
granola
sugar sprinkles
jam
French bread
sandwich bread
barbecue sauce

Dairy

butter or margarine
milk or almond milk
heavy whipping cream
cream cheese
eggs
shredded cheddar/
    jack cheese mix
Parmesan cheese
feta cheese
yogurt
ice cream

Herbs and Spices

salt
pepper
garlic powder
curry powder
dried oregano
dried basil
fresh mint
dried lavender
cinnamon
chives

Fruits and Vegetables

lemon
lime
assorted berries
Bartlett pears
pomegranate
stone fruit - peach,
    plum or apricot
butter lettuce
spinach
red onion
celery
cucumber
avocado
potato

Poultry, Meat and Fish

Italian sausage
smoked salmon
chicken breast
bacon

Alcoholic Beverages

Prosecco
rum
Baileys

Miscellaneous

ice
toothpicks
edible flowers

How to make a perfect cuppa!

The key to making a perfect cup of tea is boiling water!

This is not hot water boiled in a microwave, or hot water straight from the tap. It is hot water boiled either on a stove top or in an electric kettle. The water should be at a rolling, bubbling boil, and then it's ready to pour over loose tea or a tea bag. This makes a perfect cuppa!

If you are brewing tea in a teapot, then add more loose tea or tea bags and let it steep before pouring.

Here we go ...

- Bring the water to a boil.

- Have your tea bag or 1 teaspoon of tea leaves ready in the cup.

- If making tea in a teapot, have approximately 3 to 4 teaspoons of tea leaves ready in the teapot.

- Pour the boiling water into the cup or teapot.

- Allow to steep for 2 to 3 minutes in the teacup or 4 to 5 minutes in the teapot.

- Remove the tea bag. If making a black tea add warm milk if you choose to at this time. Sweeten with your desired sweetener.

- If you prefer your tea without milk you can add a squeeze of fresh lemon juice instead.

- Traditional black tea flavors that contain the Chamillia Sinensis tea leaf: English Breakfast, Earl Grey and Darjeeling caffeinated and decaffeinated.

- Caffeine-free herbal tisanes and infusions: Chamomile, Rooibos/Red Bush and Mint.

Perkins Park, Pacific Grove

Teatime

Growing up in England prior to global warming was a fitting precursor for my love of tea. My parents had emigrated from Jamaica, at the time still a British colony, to England in the 1950s. They have shared many a story of that transition and adjusting to life in a cold climate. It is no surprise that within days they were drinking tea. The bone-chilling damp of a West Midlands' winter will have you sipping on a hot cuppa each time you return from the frigid outdoors. I notice in England one tends to drink tea like water. The caffeine does not always play a part; dedicated tea drinkers imbibe all day long with nary a problem.

As I was born in England, unlike my parents I grew up seeing everyone put the kettle on both at home and when visiting friends, a daily ritual of sorts. I recall making my first cup of tea at the age of nine. While visiting my sister in London, I decided to make her some tea and I proudly presented her with a cup of orange liquid. We still laugh about it!

Queen Elizabeth is said to enjoy her daily afternoon cup of Earl Grey and teatime foods to this day. Let's just say Her Majesty knows a good thing. My description of middle-class tea drinking, as described above, is very different to the rituals of Queen Elizabeth and Anna Russell, the 7th Duchess of Bedford and a dear friend of Queen Victoria. Anna's claim to fame is that she created the tradition of Afternoon Tea.

Dinner in the early nineteenth century was usually served well into the evening. Anna began enjoying a cup of Darjeeling tea along with sandwiches and small cakes as a little pick me up in the afternoon. It offset the hunger that lingered while waiting for the late dinner – and hence the birth of Afternoon Tea.

Today, I personally find teatime to be a time spent relaxing, and treating oneself to a kind moment in a quiet spot sipping on a mug of tea with a nice cookie. It's a good way to celebrate a birthday, shower or other special occasion with family and friends.

Teatime Menus

Here is a list of the various types of teatime foods along with the recipes from this book that you can make to savor them.

CREAM TEA – enjoy any time of day.
Scones, Lemon Curd, Scone Cream and tea of choice.

AFTERNOON TEA – traditionally enjoyed at 4 p.m.
Anytime that suits is fine, though.
Tea Sandwiches, Scones, Lemon Curd, Scone Cream, Queen Cakes, Butter Cookies, Strawberry Lemonade and tea of choice.

HIGH TEA – traditionally enjoyed at 5 or 6 p.m.
Nowadays high tea is ideal for brunch and can be enjoyed any time of day.
TeaMosa, Celery Leaf Soup, Butter Lettuce Salad, Tea Sandwiches, Sausage Rolls, Spinach Quiche, Scones, Lemon Curd, Scone Cream, Chocolate Queen Cake and tea of choice.

EDDISON & MELROSE Party Favorites
In addition to the recipes above, these are enjoyed within many celebratory menus.
Everyday Parfait, Soirée Parfait, French Toast Bites, Joan's Kickin' Chickin' and MoTeaTo.

Celebrate!

Photo by Debby Beck

Photo by Debby Beck

Photo by Andrew Murray

Tea Table Recipes

Queen Cake (not all flowers pictured here are edible).

Celery Leaf Soup

Makes 8 C soup

2 Tbsp olive oil

½ C finely diced red onion

1 C chopped celery leaves

2 C chopped celery stalks

2 C water

1 tsp salt

3 C peeled and diced russet potatoes

4 C vegetable broth

2 tsp olive oil

salt to taste

8 celery leaves

Optional: 2 Tbsp cream

You will need 2 medium saucepans, cutting board, chopping knife and blender.

1. Warm the olive oil in the saucepan.

2. Add the red onion, celery leaves and celery stalks, sauté on medium heat for 5 minutes.

3. Add 2 C of water. Cover and simmer for 15 to 20 minutes.

4. Stir in the salt, potatoes and vegetable broth.

5. Cover and simmer for 30 minutes more.

6. Turn off the heat and transfer the soup 2 C at a time into the blender. Drizzle in a portion of the 2 tsp of the olive oil prior to blending. Hold the lid down on the blender with a kitchen towel, do not leave the blender unattended while in use. Blend until smooth.

7. Transfer the blended soup into the second saucepan.

8. Once all the soup and olive oil is blended together and placed in the second saucepan, add salt to taste.

9. Serve in teacups garnished with the celery leaf on the side.

10. If using cream, drizzle on the top of each serving.

If you have leftovers this stores well in the freezer.

Butter Lettuce Salad

Serves 4

2 heads of butter lettuce

1 C crumbled feta

½ C pomegranate seeds

2 Bartlett pears

4 Tbsp walnut pieces

Your choice of oil and vinegar to drizzle on top.

You will need a medium bowl, paper towels (or salad spinner) small knife and 4 salad plates.

1. Wash and dry the lettuce using either a salad spinner or pat the leaves dry with paper towels.

2. Set aside 4 whole lettuce leaves for garnishing.

3. Break the remaining leaves into bite-size pieces.

4. Put two heaping cups of the lettuce on each salad plate.

5. Sprinkle each plate with the feta, walnuts and pomegranate.

6. Place the reserved whole lettuce leaf on the side of each plate. Core each pear to remove the seeds. Slice each pear in half. Cut each half into 4 to 6 slices and arrange on top of the whole lettuce leaf as shown.

7. Drizzle each salad with oil and vinegar.

A lovely light, seasonal salad.

A perfect accompaniment!

Lovers Point, Pacific Grove

Sausage Rolls

Makes 4 large or 16 mini rolls

2 C all-purpose flour

¼ tsp salt

½ C olive oil

½ C cold water

4 individual 5-inch mild Italian sausages

½ C all-purpose flour for dusting

1 Tbsp olive oil for brushing

½ C mustard for service

You will need a medium bowl, measuring tape, cookie sheet brushed lightly with olive oil, rolling pin, pastry brush and medium chef's knife.

Preheat oven to 425 degrees.

1. Using a medium bowl combine the flour and salt. Add the olive oil and water to the flour mixture.

2. Rub together to form a dough.

3. Dust a clean work surface with flour. Roll the dough into a square measuring approximately 10 x 10 inch.

4. Cut the pastry into 4 equal squares.

5. Place one sausage horizontally on one pastry square. Roll to cover the sausage from end to end and place on the lightly greased cookie sheet.

6. Repeat for the remaining sausages to total 4 rolls.

7. For 4 large rolls: make 3 angled incisions on the top of each roll.

8. For mini rolls: cut each length into fourths.

9. Brush each roll with olive oil. Bake at 425 degrees for 15 to 20 minutes.

Serve with mustard on the side.

Tea Sandwiches

These little gems may be as extravagant or simplistic as you would like.

Having made thousands of mini tea sandwiches, I will warn you that they can be more work than one realizes, just ask my brother. Here, I am sharing with you the easiest of methods to cut, fill and assemble.

1. To keep cutting easy use a cookie cutter rather than a bread knife.

2. Have your sandwich fillings ready prior to cutting the bread.

3. If using a bread knife, keep a damp cloth close by to wipe your knife after making your cuts which will give a clean edge to the sandwiches.

4. Cover the sandwiches with plastic wrap once they are ready to prevent them from drying out. Do not uncover them until you are ready to serve.

5. Think of something edible and pretty to garnish your tea sandwiches with, such as fresh chives or edible flowers.

6. Serve them on a beautiful plate or stand.

7. Use a variety of breads. Sandwiches may be prepared closed with two slices of bread or open faced where there is only one slice of the bread on the bottom but not on the top.

8. Get creative with the fillings. I have provided recipes for a few of my popular flavors. Children are often a great source for ideas. Ask them what they would like and let them guide you. Of course, the same goes for grownups too. Find out the favorite foods of your guests to incorporate and help create your own unique, tasty gems.

Remember to save the crusts from your trimmed sandwich bread. Those trimmings are perfect for the fresh breadcrumb recipe I have included on page 28.

Sandwich Fillings

In addition to the recipes I have included, these are some other items that may be used:

- smoked salmon
- ham
- bacon lettuce and tomato
- egg salad
- avocado cheddar

Curried Chicken Salad Tea Sandwich Filling

Makes 8 to 12 mini tea sandwiches

   1 C diced cooked chicken breast

   ¾ C diced ripe avocado

   2 Tbsp raisins

   1 tsp salt

   2 tsp curry powder

You will need a food processor and spatula.

1. Place all ingredients in the food processor and process for 30 seconds until combined.
2. Scrape the sides and process for 10 seconds more.
3. Spread onto your bread of choice as a sandwich filling.

Cucumber Cream Cheese Tea Sandwiches

Makes 12 mini tea sandwiches

24 2-inch cookie cutter circles of sandwich bread

½ C cream cheese

24 skinny slices of English cucumber

You will need a cutting board and sandwich spreader.

1. Spread the 24 circles of bread with the cream cheese.
2. Add 2 slices of cucumber to 12 of the bread circles.
3. Place the remaining 12 circles on top to finish the 12 mini tea sandwiches.

Sundried Tomato Bacon Tea Sandwich Filling

Makes 12 mini sandwiches

½ C cooked crispy bacon, crumbled

1 Tbsp sundried tomatoes

½ C cream cheese

You will need a food processor.

1. Break the cream cheese into sections and place in the food processor.

2. Add the bacon and sundried tomatoes.

3. Process for 30 seconds until smooth and creamy.

4. Use as a sandwich filling, enjoy on toast or combine with other sandwich fixings.

Big Sur

Monterey Bay

Joan's Kickin' Chickin' (JKC)

Makes 20 mini chicken bites

20 uncooked 1-inch cubes of chicken breast, seasoned with a dash of salt, ¼ tsp lemon zest, 1 tsp lemon juice and 1 tsp olive oil

1 C fresh breadcrumbs

1 Tbsp Parmesan cheese

¼ tsp dried basil

1 Tbsp olive oil (x2)

1 Tbsp butter (x2)

Optional: barbecue sauce

You will need a medium-size frying pan, tongs, 2 bowls, paper towels, serving platter and toothpicks.

1. Combine the breadcrumbs, Parmesan and basil in a bowl.

2. Warm the first batch of 1 Tbsp of olive oil and 1 Tbsp of butter in the pan.

3. Add 10 seasoned chicken cubes to the crumb mixture and coat gently on all sides.

4. Brown the breaded chicken pieces in the pan for 3 minutes per side.

5. Once cooked through and golden brown place on a paper towel and pat dry.

6. Remove the pan from the heat and wipe clean with a paper towel. Repeat steps 2 to 5 with the remaining 10 cubes of chicken.

7. Discard any remaining crumb mixture.

This recipe is inspired by my dear friend Chef Joan. We stood side by side in the kitchen many times.

One of my favorite memories is watching her make a chicken dish similar to this one after plucking a lemon ... from her tree. She loved lemons, as I do.

Enjoy plain or with a side of barbecue sauce.

Fresh Breadcrumbs

4 C bread crusts (saved from tea sandwich and French bread trimmings)

Preheat oven to 400 degrees.

You will need a cookie sheet, food processor, bowl or storage container / bag.

1. Arrange the bread crusts on the cookie sheet.

2. Bake 15 to 20 minutes until golden and crispy.

3. Allow to cool for 15 minutes.

4. Process in the food processor until fine. Some pieces may be slightly larger and that's all right.

Set aside in a bowl to use for this recipe. The crumbs may also be stored in a freezer in an airtight container or bag for up to 3 months.

Flowers pictured are not edible and are for garnish only.

Spinach Quiche

Serves 6 to 8

2 C all-purpose flour

¼ tsp salt

½ C olive oil

½ C cold water

6 eggs

1 tsp salt

¼ tsp: black pepper, garlic powder and oregano

2 C chopped spinach

1½ C milk

1½ C shredded cheddar jack cheese mix

½ C all-purpose flour for dusting

1 Tbsp olive oil for brushing

You will need a medium-size bowl, rolling pin, whisk and medium size pie plate lightly greased with olive oil.

Preheat oven to 425 degrees.

1. Mix the flour and salt together in a medium bowl. Add the olive oil and water to the flour mixture.

2. Rub together to form a dough.

3. Dust a clean work surface with flour. Roll the dough into the shape and size of the pie plate you are using.

4. Lift the pastry and place into the pie plate. Pinch the edges of the pastry over the rim of the plate to form a crust.

5. Wash and dry the bowl. Add the eggs. salt, pepper, garlic powder and oregano.

6. Add the spinach, milk and cheese. Whisk together until all ingredients are blended. Pour the mixture into the pastry-lined pie plate.

7. Brush the pastry crust with 1 tablespoon of olive oil.

8. Bake at 425 degrees for 20 to 25 minutes until golden brown with crisp pastry edges.

9. Allow to cool for 30 minutes prior to serving.

E&M Heart-Smart Lemon Curd

Makes ½ C curd

½ C fresh lemon juice

1 Tbsp finely grated lemon zest

2 Tbsp all-purpose flour

¾ C sugar

You will need a zester, whisk, strainer, small bowl and small saucepan.

1. Whisk all the ingredients together in a small bowl.

2. Transfer to a small sauce pan.

3. Whisk as the liquid comes to a boil, reduce heat, simmer and whisk for 1 minute more.

4. Remove from the stove and pour through a strainer.

5. Transfer into your small service cup or bowl.

6. Allow to cool for 30 minutes or more before serving.

7. Enjoy with scones or toast.

E&M West Coast Scones

Makes 8 scones

2 C all-purpose flour

1½ Tbsp baking powder

Pinch of salt

¼ C sugar

3 oz or ¾ stick of cold butter

1 egg

½ C milk

1 tsp of vanilla flavoring

Optional: ½ C of blueberries, raspberries or blackberries

½ C of all-purpose flour for dusting

1 tsp of sugar for sprinkling on top

You will need a grater with medium holes, rolling pin, spatula, 2 ½ inch size cookie cutter and a large cookie sheet lightly greased with butter.

Preheat oven to 425 degrees.

1. Combine the first four ingredients in a large bowl.

2. Grate the cold butter into the bowl with the other ingredients. Rub together with your fingers until the mixture is crumbled.

3. In a small bowl whisk the egg, milk and vanilla together.

4. Pour the liquid into the dry crumb mixture.

5. Using a spatula gently mix the ingredients together until a soft dough is formed. If making a fruit scone add your fruit now and mix in gently.

6. Dust your clean board or counter top with flour and roll the dough to a ¾ inch thickness.

7. Using the cookie cutter cut 8 scones and place 2 inches apart on the cookie sheet. Sprinkle the top of each scone with the teaspoon of sugar.

8. Bake for 5 minutes, after 5 minutes turn the tray around and bake for a further 5 to 7 minutes until nicely browned.

Allow to cool for 10 to 15 minutes.
Enjoy with butter, jam, curd, cream or solo.

Scone Cream

Makes enough for 8 to 12 scones

1   C heavy whipping cream

½   C powdered sugar

You will need a medium bowl and electric whisk or stand-up mixer, spatula and serving cup.

1. Place the ingredients in bowl. Whisk together for 3 to 5 minutes until stiff peaks are formed.

2. Spoon into your serving cup and serve with scones and lemon curd.

This is a quick and easy version of the cream I use to serve along with scones. Clotted Cream, a specialty of Devonshire, England is traditionally used, but it takes a while to make. It is also heavier, although delicious. This version pairs perfectly with the buttery scone recipe and is lighter and less time-consuming than traditional Clotted Cream.

Queen Cakes

Makes 1 medium round Queen Cake or
12 small Queen Cakes

1¼ C all-purpose flour

1 C room temperature butter

¾ C sugar

1 tsp baking powder

½ tsp salt

3 eggs

1 tsp vanilla

1 Tbsp lemon juice

Chocolate Cake version

Omit the lemon juice
In addition you will need:

½ C cocoa powder

¼ C milk

You will need a mixing bowl, wooden spoon, spatula, cake pan of choice and cooking spray.

Preheat oven to 350 degrees.

1. Using a wooden spoon mix the butter and sugar together in the bowl until creamy in texture.

2. Add the eggs, vanilla and lemon juice (no lemon juice if making the chocolate cake). Mix until smooth.

3. Add the flour, salt and baking powder. Mix until smooth.

4. If making the chocolate cake, mix in the cocoa powder and then the milk until smooth.

5. Spray the cake or cupcake pan with cooking spray and spoon the mixture evenly into the pan(s).

6. Bake the cupcakes at 350 degrees for 15 minutes. Bake the whole cake for 25 to 30 minutes.

Allow to cool for 30 minutes before removing from the pan and decorating.

This buttery not-too-sweet cake mix is versatile and delicious. Use any frosting of your choice to decorate. Keep it basic or add berries, sprinkles, chocolate shavings and/or edible flowers to spruce it up. Create and be playful!

Queen Cake Cream

Makes 1 pint – enough to decorate a medium Queen Cake or 12 small Queen Cakes

1 pint heavy whipping cream

1 C powdered sugar

Optional: splash of food coloring of choice

Chocolate Cake version

Add ½ C cocoa powder

You will need a mixing bowl, electric whisk or stand-up mixer, spatula, piping nozzle and piping bag.

1. Add the ingredients to the bowl.

2. Whisk together for 3 to 5 minutes until stiff peaks are formed.

3. Use to spread on your cake with a spatula or put into a piping bag with nozzle attached to decorate.

An incredibly easy recipe that tastes delicious and adds a fine touch to your cake. Best when decorated just before serving. When making in advance keep the items refrigerated to prevent the cream from melting.

Editor Josie enjoying a tea break.

Butter Cookies

1 C all-purpose flour

½ C butter (room temp)

1½ Tbsp powdered sugar

1½ Tbsp sugar

Pinch of salt

½ C all-purpose flour for dusting

Your choice of 1 Tbsp of finely chopped lavender or 2 Tbsp of crunchy sugar sprinkles to sprinkle on top of each cookie.

You will need a mixing bowl, rolling pin, 2½ inch size cookie cutter, and a medium to large ungreased cookie sheet.

Preheat oven to 325 degrees.

1. Combine the first 5 ingredients in a large bowl.

2. Using your fingers crumble the ingredients together.

3. If using the lavender add it at this time.

4. Continue to work the ingredients until a soft dough is formed.

5. Dust your clean work surface with flour and roll the dough to a ¼ inch thickness.

6. Using the cookie cutter cut 8-12 cookies. Place 2 inches apart on the cookie sheet. If using the crunchy sugar sprinkles, sprinkle each cookie with the sugar at this time.

7. Bake for 15 to 20 minutes until the cookies are barely golden and firm.

Allow to cool for 30 minutes or more before serving.

These not-too-sweet cookies are perfect with a nice cup of tea. Rich, crumbly treats that are ideal for decorating and dressing up in so many ways. Have fun with these!

Karen Anne's Everyday Granola Parfait

Serves 4

2 C vanilla or other yogurt of choice

2 C fresh berries (or frozen and thawed berries) and/or sliced bananas

1 C E&M's Karen Anne's Granola (or other gourmet brand)

Toppings: 4 tsp honey or maple syrup

You will need 4 teacups or bowls.

Add to each: ½ C of yogurt, ½ C berries and/or bananas and sprinkle with ¼ C of granola. Drizzle with 1 tsp of honey or maple syrup. Enjoy!

Karen Anne's Soiree Granola Parfait!

Serves 4

2 C vanilla ice cream or other ice cream of choice

2 C fresh berries or finely diced stone fruit (peach, plum, apricot...)

1 C E&M's Karen Anne's Granola (or other gourmet brand)

Optional toppings: 1 Tbsp each of whipped cream, and/or Baileys, fresh mint leaves for garnish

You will need 4 teacups, martini or wine glasses.

Add to each: ½ C of ice cream, ½ C berries or diced stone fruit, and sprinkle with ¼ C of granola. Top with 1 Tbsp of whipped cream and, if using, drizzle with 1 Tbsp of Baileys. Garnish with a sprig of mint. Enjoy!

These parfaits are easy and fun! The Everyday option is ideal for breakfast or a snack. The Soiree option is a quick and tasty finishing touch to a dinner party.

French Toast Bites

16 cubes of French Bread, crusts removed, (may be saved to make breadcrumb recipe on page 28) approximation 1¼ inch in diameter.

1½ C milk

2 eggs

1 tsp vanilla

¼ tsp cinnamon

2 Tbsp of olive oil or butter

2 Tbsp powdered sugar

¼ C maple syrup

You will need a medium bowl, large frying pan, whisk, tongs, serving dish and a sifter.

Preheat oven to 325 degrees.

1. Whisk the milk, eggs, vanilla and cinnamon together in a bowl.

2. Heat the oil or butter gently in a frying pan on the stove.

3. Gradually add 4 cubes of bread at a time to the liquid. Allow the bread to absorb the liquid.

4. Add the cubes of bread to the frying pan 4 at a time to total 8 per batch.

5. Turn the cubes over once browned and gradually brown all sides.

6. Pour the maple syrup into the serving dish. Add the first batch of browned cubes and put into the oven to keep warm.

7. Repeat with the remaining 8 cubes of bread by dipping into the liquid and browning in the pan. Add more oil or butter if necessary.

8. Add to the serving dish and finish with a dusting of powdered sugar.

Perfect for a breakfast or brunch addition to your table.

We never know when we become inspired! The tiniest thing can lead to something new, as it was with this recipe that I came up with. My son was experiencing some discomfort after his orthodontist appointment. By removing the crust from the bread, these soft bites became a hit – and a unique morning addition to the table.

Strawberry Lemonade

Serves 4

1 C strawberries (fresh or frozen) washed, stems removed

½ C sugar

1 C cold water

2 Tbsp fresh-squeezed lemon juice

4 C ice

1 C cold water

You will need a saucepan, spoon, blender, strainer, pitcher and 4 glasses.

1. Place the first 3 ingredients in a saucepan and bring to a boil.
2. Allow to simmer for 15 minutes.
3. Remove from the stove and stir in the lemon juice.
4. Cool for 15 minutes.
5. Pour the liquid into the blender, add 1 cup of cold water and blend until smooth.
6. Place the strainer over the pitcher and pour the liquid through.
7. Add 1 C of ice to each glass.
8. Add the second cup of cold water to the pitcher and stir.
9. Pour the lemonade into each glass.

Truly a kid favorite!

This fruity lemonade brings out the summertime kid in all of us regardless of the time of year.

The E&M MoTeaTo

Makes 4 to 6 servings

½ C fresh-squeezed lime juice

4 Tbsp white sugar

3 C boiling water

1 C steeped regular or decaf tea of choice

Your choice of:

 1 C white rum OR 1 C of sparkling water

4 C ice

4 to 6 slices of lime

12 sprigs of fresh mint

You will need a medium-size saucepan, pitcher or glass jug, whisk, tea cups or glasses to serve.

1. Combine the first 3 ingredients in a saucepan and whisk together until the sugar is dissolved.
2. Add the steeped tea and transfer to a pitcher or glass jug.
3. Rub 6 sprigs of mint with your fingers to release the essence and add to the mixture.
4. If using rum add it at this time. Pour into the tea cups or glasses, add the ice.
5. If using sparkling water pour the mixture into the tea cups or glasses and add the ice. Pour a portion of sparkling water into each serving.
6. Finish with a slice of lime gently squeezed and a sprig of mint.

TeaMosa

Serves 4

4 ⅓ C chilled brewed tea of choice

Optional: sweeten with sugar or honey

4 ⅓ C Prosecco

You will need 4 champagne glasses.

1.   Pour ⅓ C of tea into each champagne glass

2.   Add ⅓ C of Prosecco

Cheers!

Fort Ord Dunes State Park

Contributors

Author, Chef, Photographer Karen Anne

Photo by Sheila Saam

was born and raised in the West Midlands, England. 2021 marks Karen's 35th year of being a chef. Today she lives with her family in California and is the proprietress of Eddison & Melrose Tea Cottage.

Asilomar Dunes.

Photo by Jesse Gabriel Photography

Editor and food tester Josie Cowden is from Yorkshire, England, where she developed a taste for afternoon tea and scones. She now lives in the Santa Cruz area in California where she writes about food and wine. Having traveled to more than 75 counties, she has garnered a wealth of experience in cuisines of the world, but still enjoys a simple cup of tea and a piece of shortbread.

Photographer Sophia Sorenson is a Pacific Grove native who now resides in the Bay Area after attending Arizona State University. She would rather be behind the camera than in front. She loves the beach and spending time with her family.

Photos by Dale Ramos

CPSIA information can be obtained
at www.ICGtesting.com
Printed in the USA
BVHW020443240922
647824BV00002B/15